Miramont Park
and Other Poems

poems by

John Paul McKinney

Finishing Line Press
Georgetown, Kentucky

Miramont Park
and Other Poems

For Kathy

ACKNOWLEDGMENTS

I would like to acknowledge with sincere gratitude the help and guidance
that I have received over the past few years from my mentor and friend,
Angela Alaimo O'Donnell, who has read and commented on my poetry,
and given me the same support and direction that she offers in her writing
classes to the fortunate students at Fordham University.

In addition, I want to acknowledge the kind consideration of Jill Peláez
Baumgaertner, poetry editor at *The Christian Century*, in which one of these
poems, "Mary Had a Little Lamb," was published.

The architectural layout of Miramont Park is the combined work of the City
of Fort Collins Departments of Parks Planning and Art in Public Places with
design features by the renowned artist, Andy Dufford.

Publisher: Leah Huete de Maines
Editor: Christen Kincaid
Cover Photo: John Paul McKinney
Author Photo: Kathleen G. McKinney
Cover Design: Elizabeth Maines McCleavy

Order online: www.finishinglinepress.com
also available on amazon.com

Author inquiries and mail orders:
Finishing Line Press
PO Box 1626
Georgetown, Kentucky 40324
USA

Table of Contents

Miramont Park

These fourteen poems constitute a corona of sonnets, written during the first year of the corona virus. They record life on a small city park near our home in Fort Collins, Colorado.

1. The Generous Hill in Mourning

The generous hill is quiet this morning,
alone and naked, covered only with a blanket of snow,
snow that's marked by yesterday's sleighs and tiny feet,
slide marks of sleds, discs and plastic sheets

where yesterday's children screamed and laughed,
and 3rd grade dare devils displayed their skills
for giggling, brightly colored winter-clad ladies
of about the same age.

But yesterday's children are all gone now,
obediently sheltered in place in the face
of a deadly virus
that has silenced their play.

The generous hill is quiet this morning,
alone and naked, covered only with a blanket of snow.

2. An old man continues his walk

Alone and naked, covered only with a blanket of snow,
the park is abandoned by all but a few pairs of geese
and a random old man limping along the trail
till he passes a child on a bike, so standing apart

he lets the bike pass
before he goes back to his walk,
his pace deliberate, clunk after clunk,
each step measured as he bobs along.

Does he keep life together
by walking each morning like this?
Is he counting his steps?
Are his days also numbered?

I stare at the park, each morning the same.
The days roll out without number or name.

3. Days without number, weeks without end

The days roll out without number or name.
It matters little;
There is no appointment with the dentist at 4:00
nor a schedule to pick up the children from school.

The days are all equal, like squares on a patchwork
quilt, a "crazy quilt" of days and weeks
when we have to remind ourselves
when to go to bed and when to eat.

The hours, like days, have an unsettling way
of merging from one to the next.
What matters now is not when but how
do we manage to keep ourselves safe?

Safe from an enemy, safe from our friends
by staying apart, we are closer.

4. A Walk in the Park

One touch of nature makes the whole world kin
—Shakespeare

By staying apart, we are closer,
knowing our love for each other,
keeping our distance, standing apart
from strangers, neighbors, or brothers.

On a walk through the park, I notice ahead
a couple coming quickly my way.
We get off the sidewalk, each to their right,
I to one side, they to the other.

"It's as if we don't care for each other," I jokingly yell.
"No, but we do," comes his answer.
"We both want you to be well.
Y que tengas un buen día, amigo."

Yes, have a good day, my new friend,
I hope that I'll see you again.

5. On meeting again

I hope that I'll see you again
when this bug is reduced to a fading footnote
in a medical journal, and the world breathes free.
Yes, I hope that I'll see you again.

Perhaps we can have a cerveza together
and cheer for the Rockies.
I'll learn more words in your idioma;
We'll mix it up with English and Spanish.

But if we don't meet up again—
you may succumb, or so might I—
I'll look for you in the parks of heaven
taking our walk—I'll see you then.

So, either way, my new-found friend
this virus has brought us together.

6. A living paradox

Cor ad cor loquitur. (Heart speaks to heart).
Motto of Saint John Henry Cardinal Newman

This virus has brought us together
across our towns throughout the country,
across the miles and into the homes
of friends and cousins who live far away.

Thankful for Edison, Alexander G. Bell,
for J.C.R. Lickliter and all
the researchers at MIT and UCLA
who paved the way,

who made it possible for us to stay
connected via telephone, the internet,
face time, skype, zoom
and yes, the US mail.

So, though we may be miles apart
we're closer than ever, heart to heart.

7. Neighbors; Magnified

We're closer than ever, heart to heart
and more of what we've always been.
The gentle lady down the street
is kinder than ever to those she meets.

Mr. Grumpy (as the neighborhood kids
call him behind his back)
is grumpier still from being cooped up
not by choice, but forced decree.

The young mother of teen-age twins,
who volunteers at church and school,
has offered to pick up groceries for
all the elderly who can't—or shouldn't—go out.

This coronavirus appears to pass
as nature's magnifying glass.

8. Becoming

As nature's magnifying glass,
focusing on our virtues and faults,
the virus presses an invitation
to see and become our better selves.

And when it brings soft light to bear,
see there the good in sharp relief
against a grey bokeh of flaws
that fade into the hazy past.

We put on masks for our daily walk
protecting one another from germs
We'll take off these and other masks
When we feel completely safe together.

When this is over, can we ever be
the people we were meant to be?

9. My brother's death

In memory of George Floyd

The people we were meant to be
are challenged now by an enemy,
mortally stronger than deadly virus,
fueling hatred, based on race.

Murder on the street, twisted, grotesque,
a cop's slow murder of an other
not like me, but other
As if he were not, in fact, my brother.

My brother is black, and I am white;
part of the same family since birth.
Teachers liked me; they didn't like him
I got new stuff, he got leftovers.

And now he is dead and I am alive.
His final words still pierce my ears.

10. Dying words

His final words still pierce my ears
and rattle around inside my head
reverberating down the alleyways
of centuries, searing and stinging.

I hear them echoing as I smell the salt
of his sweat and the sticky blood
still on his cheek and head
I hear them echoing down the years:

I can't breathe . . . *I thirst.*
Momma, momma . . . *Abba.*
Everything hurts . . . *Why hast thou abandoned me?*
They're going to kill me . . . *It is finished.*

They killed my brother and now
this world will never be the same.

11. Hope

This world will never be the same,
yet youth will press to make it so,
at least to have a chance to win
their coming battles in their own brave way.

This morning the generous hill is host
to ten or twelve young girls and boys,
in training for sports as they briskly run
sideways up to the peak and back.

Tentative at first, still keeping
social distance prescribed by law
they stretch and twist, then dash their way
across the field and up the hill.

Their coach then whistles their practice over
as thunder rolls across the field.

12. Spring

As thunder rolls across the field
the few remaining geese in pairs
wander to the pond to meet
the others with their chicks in tow.

Beneath the cloud of coronavirus
and now of riots in the street
with major stealth and no prior notice
spring has crept into Miramont Park.

A child runs up the hill, rolls down;
oblivious to the impending storm,
runs up again until his mom
yells, "Time for us to go back home."

My murdered brother still on my mind:
Did our Mother call my brother home?

13. A question looking for an answer

Did our Mother call my brother home,
and did She have a hug for him,
kiss his sweaty head, and wipe
away his earthborn salty tears?

Still other questions here below
scream out and linger in the air
like fog that cannot clear itself
as crowds engorge and their voices swell.

Is this the moment? Is this the time,
the first time in my eighty-five years
when my black brothers will get good stuff
and be loved as much as white brothers and me?

No answer is given, the fog remains.
I must create the answer myself.

14. An answer lies in Miramont Park

I must create the answer myself
but I'll never have to create it alone.
The park is quietly coming to life.
The old man with his cane clunks by.

A skateboarder just misses the Mexican couple.
The black Bahamian Olympic jumper,
clears the park bench in one sudden leap,
signaling courage and a leap of faith.

Faith yes, hope Yes, love, YES!
Aha, my answer starts right here
with blocks as basic as the Stonehenge
blocks on the crest of the hill. I'll start here.

Surveying the scene like a full mother waiting,
the generous hill is quiet this morning.

A Slew of Sunday Sonnets

Mad Millie

Each Sunday Millie, somber, pale, and thin,
dissects the sermon from her front row post,
then skyward whispers words with knowing grin
and giggles softly to an unseen Host.

And when the congregation joins the choir
she cranes her neck and smiling, hands held high,
assumes she should be drawn up even higher,
like Mary, hoisted straight into the sky.

With whom does Millie chat with such desire?
"Hallucinations" expert doctors say.
But face and figure full of heaven's fire
another explanation do betray:

With speech that seems erratic, gestures flighty,
Mad Millie shares a joke with the Almighty.

Easter

Mary, the woman from Magdala,
in love with Jesus of Nazareth,
crushed, heart-broken, but mainly confused
I couldn't believe that he meant it...

Trudged tombward on that grey day,
with a bag of oils and a winding cloth
as clouds pressed down to squash the earth.
(None of the others had dared go near)

Soldiers asleep, she tiptoed up.
Stooping, she looked—He was gone.
He did ... He did mean it. "In three days..."
She blinked as blinding sun broke through the heavy clouds.

The ancient cloud-shroud entrapping the earth
Was ripped apart, destroyed forever.

Priestly celibacy—Two responses

Celibacy I

While pastor parses well-worn words on sin
(It's Piety on which he's overdosed)
and then, depending on the mood he's in,
invokes the Father, Son, or Holy Ghost,

he rants and raves about the sin de jour
abortion, fornication, porn's effects,
whatever else might make a soul impure
but generally equating sin with sex.

Just what would keep a man from noticing
some other sins, like public theft or lies,
hypocrisy, crass greed, or words that sting,
but choose carnality to emphasize?

Perhaps it's not that he's a prude, or lewd;
The hungry man can only think of food.

Celibacy II

The bearded, disheveled old priest in the pulpit
stretched out his arms as if to encircle
the whole congregation in one giant hug,
then lectured of Love like a man possessed:

"Love one another as I have loved you."
"For God so loved the world." "Love is truth."
"Love God above all; love your neighbor as yourself."
"For love conquers all." "But the greatest of these is love."

The child in front of me whispered clear,
"That man's in love."
"Psst. No, my dear, that man's a priest.
He cannot be in love."

No, no; she has it right; he is in love
with her, with me, his church, and God above.

Mary Had a Little Lamb
(A Meditation in Perthshire)

This morning's mountains, windy, wet, all white
and brown, are bleating from the lambs first shorn,
whose gift of self removed, appear forlorn,
while Martha spins her wheel in dawning's light.

And Martha's yarn's a gift of self, as well,
infused with sweat, her skill, and love, and tear
so I can knit a scarf for you, my dear,
A scarf wherein my self, my love, will dwell.

If lamb is gift and giver, sealed since birth
and Martha's yarn is part of Martha, too,
as well my scarf contains my love for you,
then givers may be gifts throughout the earth.

But whence the primal giver-gift, so pure?
It's Mary's Lamb, it's Mary's Lamb, I'm sure.

Homeless

(A Meditation at Peace House—Minneapolis, MN)

> *"The foxes have holes and the birds of the air have nests,*
> *but the Son of Man has nowhere to lay His head."*
> *Luke 9:58*

These scattered, weary, homeless ones are called
by name: Elijah, Emerald and Grace....
Here sheltered from the elements and walled
from those who cannot, will not, see their face.

From near the margins of a blinded town
(Not really theirs—but someone else's space)
the wind and rain will claim them as their own
and blow them fiercely to this sacred place.

With meditation, food, and words that ease
their faces lift. Across the room a call:
"So, Emerald, then you're a jewel," his tease.
"Oh, yes, I am." And years of baggage fall.

The wind outside has quieted and died,
but now that Wind within is magnified.

A Wedding Blessing
For Peter and Paola

Be here, O Lord, to share with us today
the joyful embarkation of these two
brave lovers. Setting sail, they look to you
as on the winds of love they make their way.

You walked upon the Sea of Galilee.
You calmed the waters in a stormy gale.
Please send them peaceful seas. Let sun prevail.
Be with them on their windward side and lee.

And when they come about at end of day
to make a final reach toward heaven's shore
be there, O Lord, to welcome them—and more—
to share their endless love. For this I pray.

Be here, O Lord, to bless them on their way
and then be there beside them, day by day.

Advent

Waiting their turn on a snow-covered hill
bold children hope, as the day grows old,
that the sled will take them all the way down
without twisting or falling, or hitting a bump.

At the base of the hill two lovers caress;
he drops to his knees in the dark and holds
the small open box, professing his love,
while waiting, waiting for her ultimate "Yes!"

Now night reveals the fingernail slice of a moon.
that thief in the sky, stealing her light from the sun
swelling and swelling, night after night
like the belly of the Woman who can no longer contain

Her audacious, urgent gift of Light
that bursts with hope to smash the dark.

Eternal Pulsation
(A Meditation on the Feast of the Sacred Heart)

The pendulum clock in the corner, tapping the seconds,
metronome sounds for a mother rocking her baby to-and-fro,
while children outside are clapping, fingers snapping
the jump rope smacking the pavement.

Others on swings, back and forth, kicking the sand like
waves lapping and slapping the beach, and belching
salty white foam on timeless rocks
over and over, now and forever and ever.

As the planet hurls itself and whirls
around and around on a dizzying pound
of light and dark, dark and light
it chases away from the devil's temptation

to sever itself from its heavenly tether,
as if it could silence the pulsing forever. Never!

The Meal

For Aryeh, in praise of his gift for understanding

We would sometimes meet at Coral Gables,
perhaps the Thai place across the street,
or rather some other place to eat.
But it wasn't just about the food.

We nourished our souls as well as bodies,
our connection, past, present, and to come,
with slow conversation. You taught me the prayer
"Baruch atah Adonai, Eloheinu Melech ha-olam...."

At the shabbat meal at your place
you blessed the wine, the challah bread
and as I had before, I said,
"It's like The Eucharist." You didn't believe.

You couldn't, of course; I didn't expect you would,
but we were filled and you understood.

Succession

Grasping one another's wrists, we forged a human chain
and tugged with all our strength, struggling, straining,
pulling successive generations out of earth, one by one,
thus, lengthening the chain.

Suddenly the guy in front of me
                                   let go.
He had kept such a powerful grip
that I fell back at his sudden release.
I could no longer see him, nor hear his report
of those in front, those in the distant fog.

Then I realized that I myself was at the fore,
wishing that the others, those that followed after,
could take his place ahead of me.

I tightened hard my grip
as new links began to form behind.

Epiphany

"Out of the mouths of infants and nurslings..."
(Matthew 21:16)

Thank you, God, for the sun;
(Small arms in circles over their heads;)
Thank you, God, for the trees;
(Little fingers wiggle upright;)
Thank you, God, for the mountains;
(Fingertips together in an inverted V;)
Thank you, God, for me;
(Arms crossed over small chests.)

Even though those years have passed
They still choose their childhood prayer at meals.
Now suddenly those words demand
A deeper thought: Thank you, God, for me?

That I even am? That you choose me to be?
With you, eternally? Yes, THANK YOU, God, for me!

Postscript

Digging for ~~worms~~, words
(After reading Seamus Heaney's poem, "Digging.")

How clearly I can still recall
The hours I spent in study hall,
Just wishing for the term to end
So I the warmer days could spend

With rod in hand and creek nearby
A can of worms and cloudless sky.
But worms got from unwilling soil,
By sweaty, aching, digging toil.

Digging, turning, breaking clumps
Inspecting all the smaller lumps
For any sign of slimy worm
Quite still before it starts to squirm.

Through clay lumps, stones, and weeds that bound
The sharp-edged shovel mostly found
The worms that I would leave behind
Looking for the larger kind.

"That one's too small; I'll let him go."
I'd throw them back so they could grow
Others, slipped away, escaped
Their fate as bait.

Stop this daydream; Back to books.
Forget the worms and barbless hooks.
Here comes the prefect down the aisle
Quick! Grab a book and read awhile.

With hand in desk, I slide a book
Out stealthily, I never look.
Oh, "Songs America Sings." Okay.
I love those songs from yesterday:

"O, Paddy dear, and did you hear;
The news that's going around;
The shamrock is forbid by law
To grow on Irish ground."

"Oh, beautiful for spacious skies
For amber waves of grain…."

Good; he's passing down the aisle
Return the book into the pile…
But wait; those words…their sudden hold
With images demanding, bold.

I can do that…I can try
To unearth words that will comply
With grammar's rules and still float free
Communicating easily.

Now here I start to dig again,
Though not with shovel, but with pen
And not for worms, but words this time
Words that love to sing and rhyme

Digging deeper, digging still
Searching for the words until
I find some buried in my past
Old words perhaps to be recast.

Some slip away, some I refuse;
Still others, those I plan to use
I savor, whisper, roll them out
Or angry words that scream and shout

Bright words that ring on open air
To catch my reader unaware
To catch my reader unaware.

John Paul McKinney is a retired professor from Michigan State University, where he taught in the Departments of Psychology and Pediatrics/Human Development. His academic writing includes over 75 journal articles, chapters, and text books in psychology. His fiction includes a novel, *Charlie's Angle*, which won an EVVY award for literary fiction from the Colorado Independent Publishers' Association, two short stories, one published in *The Mountain Scribe Anthology* 2009, and the other the winner of an honorable mention in the 2008 Writers-Editors Network International Writing Competition. His poetry has appeared in *The Christian Century, St. Anthony Messenger,* and two anthologies.

He lives in Fort Collins, Colorado, with his wife, three dogs and an obnoxious parrot. When not writing or reading, he is either practicing the Celtic harp, trying to fool trout with flies in a local stream, or knitting socks or sweaters.

www.ingramcontent.com/pod-product-compliance
Lightning Source LLC
Chambersburg PA
CBHW022044080426
42734CB00009B/1226